The Joy of Bach

THE JOY OF BACH is a volume of original keyboard compositions by members of the Bach family. The history of this, the most unique clan in the annals of music, goes back to the 16th Century and reached well into the 19th, spanning a period of about 250 years.

The central towering figure of this family portrait-in-sound is, of course, Johann Sebastian Bach. It should be noted, however, that his four famous sons, represented in this collection, are also outstanding contributors to the music literature of their time. Indeed, in the 18th Century, the reputation and influence of the Bach sons had outshone that of their father. Each one of them is a strong musical personality in his own right and their works, as a whole, constitute an important bridge between the Baroque and Classical periods. In addition to Johann Sebastian and his four sons, compositions of a great-uncle and a grandson can be found in this volume. To complete the picture, a few selections from the *Little Notebook for Anna Magdalena Bach* are also included.

The pieces in THE JOY OF BACH are in their original form, neither rearranged nor simplified. Fingering, some tempo indications, dynamic and phrasing marks were added by the editor. Ornaments, for the most part, have been written out to facilitate execution.

As to the general style of performing the music of the Baroque and Rococo period, may we offer the following suggestions:
— strive for a very clear delineation of the phrasing and motivic structure;
— do not play at excessive speed, especially pieces of rich harmonic or polyphonic textures;
— avoid extreme dynamic contrasts; the range is between p and f; not between pp and ff;
— the damper pedal should be used very sparingly, mostly in "short touches";
— all ornaments are played *on the beat*, crisply and cleanly;
— finally, do not be intimidated by the pedantic rigidity of some present day scholars who consider the music of Bach as "hallowed ground" to be approached only with a college degree in musicology. The performer of the 18th Century had a great deal of freedom, fully sanctioned by the Baroque composer who did not indicate the details and nuances of execution in his manuscripts, but left it to the discretion and good taste of the player. Consequently, there are many ways to perform this music "correctly" and "in style."

Denes Agay

Order No. YK21004
US International Standard Book Number: 978.0.8256.8011.3
Library of Congress Card Catalog Number: 68-42516

Exclusive Distributors:
Hal Leonard
7777 West Bluemound Road
Milwaukee, WI 53213
Email: info@halleonard.com

Hal Leonard Europe Limited
42 Wigmore Street
Marylebone, London, W1U 2RN
Email: info@halleonardeurope.com

Hal Leonard Australia Pty. Ltd.
4 Lentara Court
Cheltenham, Victoria, 3192 Australia
Email: info@halleonard.com.au

Printed in the EU

MEMBERS OF THE BACH FAMILY

JOHANN CHRISTOPH BACH (1642-1703), a great-uncle of Johann Sebastian, was organist in Eisenach, Germany. Most of his important compositions were written for voices, but he also left a most interesting collection of 44 choral preludes one of which is presented in this folio. He was a much respected musician of his day and even decades later his famous great-nephew, Carl Philipp Emanuel wrote about him as a "great and expressive composer."

JOHANN SEBASTIAN BACH (1685-1750) one of the greatest musical minds of all times was born in Eisenach, Thuringia (Germany). He lost both his parents as a young child and was taken care of by an older brother. At the age of fifteen he began supporting himself as a choir boy. Through successive years he held positions as court violinist, church organist and, for the last thirty years of his life, as choirmaster of the renowned St. Thomas Church in Leipzig. His great number of imperishable works—oratorios, cantatas, concertos and keyboard compositions form a glorious culminating point of music's baroque period. He had twenty children of whom nine survived him. Four of his sons, represented in this volume, became outstanding composers of their time.

WILHELM FRIEDEMANN BACH (1710-1784) was the eldest and, by all accounts, the favorite son of Johann Sebastian and his first wife Maria Barbara Bach. He was ten years old when he began his formal music studies with his father's "Little Note-book for Wilhelm Friedemann Bach." The Two-and Three-voice Inventions, the "Little Preludes," the "Well-tempered Clavier" were also written mainly for his instruction. He was an extraordinarily gifted, original composer, who's somewhat unstable and restless personal life prevented the full realization of his creative powers.

CARL PHILIPP EMANUEL BACH (1714-1788), famous son of Johann Sebastian from his first marriage, lived and worked throughout most of his life in Berlin as harpsichordist at the court of Frederick the Great, and later in Hamburg as director of church music. He occupies a prominent place in the music of the 18th century as one of the originators of the classic sonata form. His keyboard works, with their rich melodic and emotional content, had a deep influence on Haydn and even Beethoven. His "Essay on the True Art of Clavier Playing" is not only one of the first important piano methods, but also a definitive source on the style and performance practices of his time.

JOHANN CHRISTOPH FRIEDRICH BACH (1732-1795), son of Johann Sebastian by his second marriage to Anna Magdalena Wülken, was for many years a court conductor in Buckeburg, Germany. His numerous compositions include oratorios, cantatas, symphonies, concertos and sonatas. His musical style, especially in his symphonies, is close to Haydn's. His shorter keyboard compositions, such as the ones in this volume, are charming, melodically most appealing period pieces.

JOHANN CHRISTIAN BACH (1735-1782), youngest son of Johann Sebastian, was, in his time, the most celebrated name in the Bach family. He was a pupil of his elder brother Carl Philipp Emanuel. Later he studied with Padre Martini in Italy. For a while he was the organist of the Milan cathedral, later he settled in London where he became extremely successful as a composer of operas. He also became music tutor to the Queen. As far as the records show, he was the first artist to give a piano recital in public, anno 1768. His keyboard compositions have a great deal of delicacy and grace, and are among the best examples of the so-called "gallant style." His works made a lasting impression on the young Mozart, who met him in London.

WILHELM FRIEDRICH ERNST BACH (1759-1845) was the son of Johann Christoph Friedrich and last male descendant of Johann Sebastian Bach. He became an accomplished instrumentalist under the tutelage of his uncle Johann Christian, in London. At the age of thirty he was appointed as royal music instructor at the court in Berlin. He composed numerous works for different instrumental combinations and, although he did not achieve the fame and success of his uncles Carl Philipp Emanuel and Johann Christian, he does represent the sixth and last generation of the remarkable Bach family with flair and dignity.

CONTENTS

Air

Wilhelm Friedemann Bach

Moderato

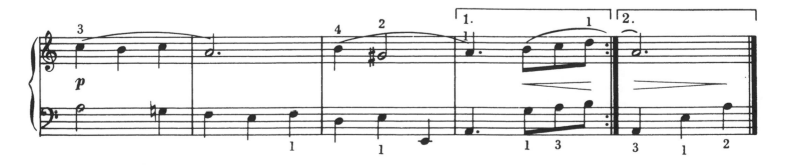

Minuet

Johann Christoph Friedrich Bach

Andantino

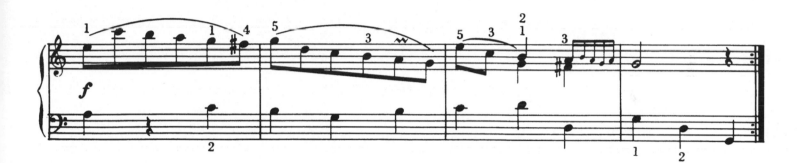

Minuet

Johann Sebastian Bach

Musette

From the Notebook for
Anna Magdalena Bach

Allegretto

Polonaise

From the Notebook for
Anna Magdalena Bach

Arioso

Andante

Carl Philipp Emanuel Bach

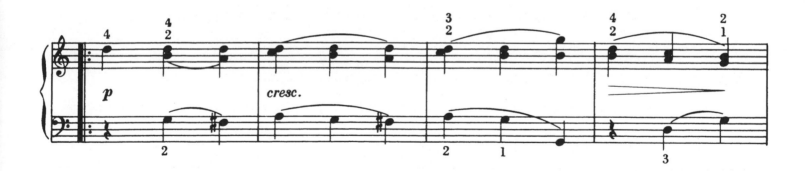

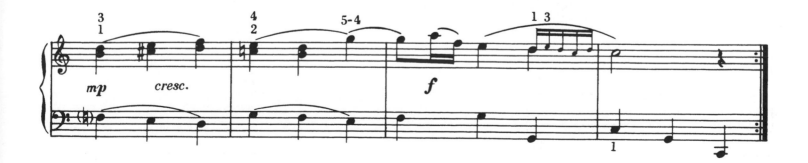

March

From the Notebook for
Anna Magdalena Bach

Moderato

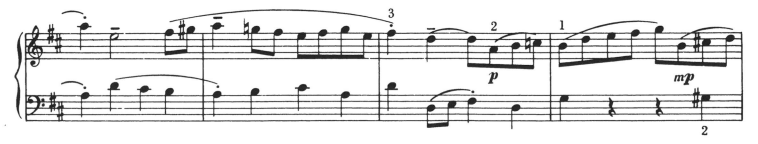

Duettino

Minuet from a Sonata in F

Wilhelm Friedemann Bach

Andante con moto

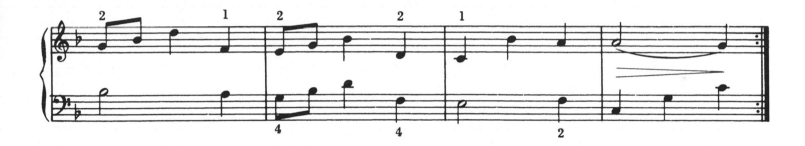

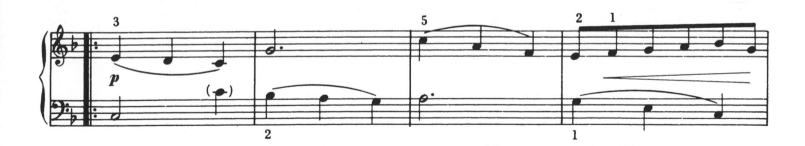

Country Dance

(Schwaebisch)

Johann Christoph Friedrich Bach

Allegretto

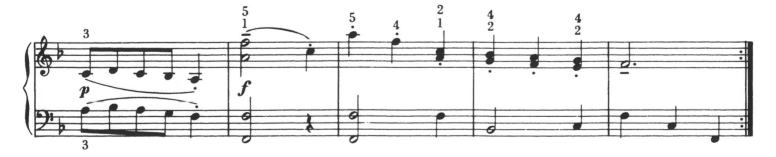

Aria

from the Notebook for Anna Magdalena Bach

Johann Sebastian Bach

Andantino cantabile

sempre legato

Allegretto Scherzando

Carl Philipp Emanuel Bach

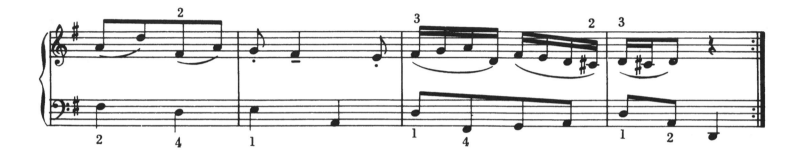

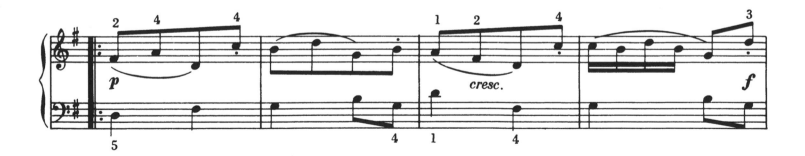

Andantino Cantabile

Carl Philipp Emanuel Bach

English Dance

Johann Christoph Friedrich Bach

* Original notation in ♩

Trio

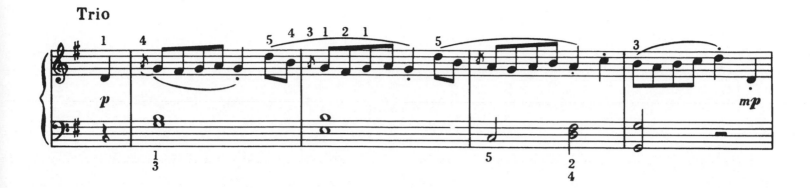

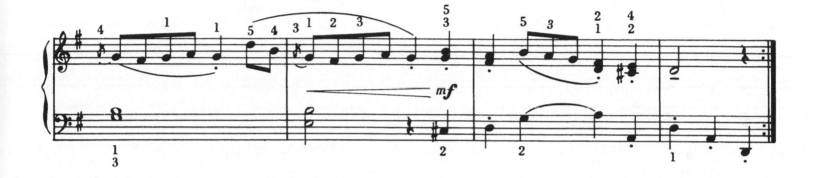

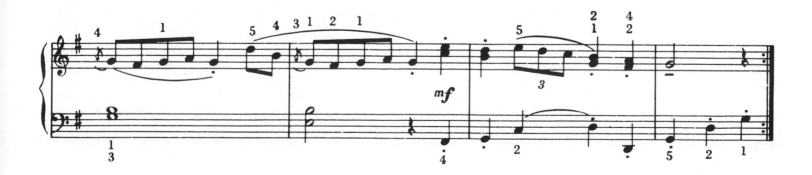

Praeludium

From The Well-Tempered Clavier

Johann Sebastian Bach

Allegro moderato

La Sybille

Carl Philipp Emanuel Bach

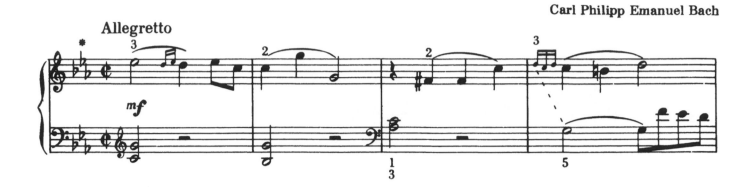

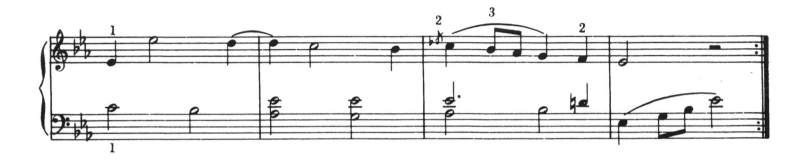

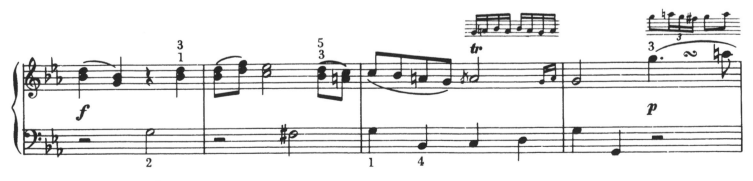

* *original key is C# minor*

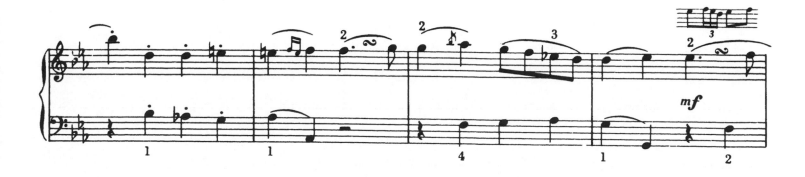

Two Waltzes

1

Wilhelm Friedrich Ernst Bach
(1759 - 1845)

Allegretto grazioso

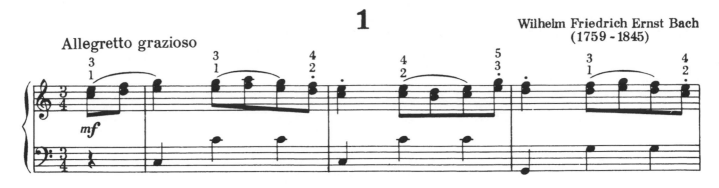

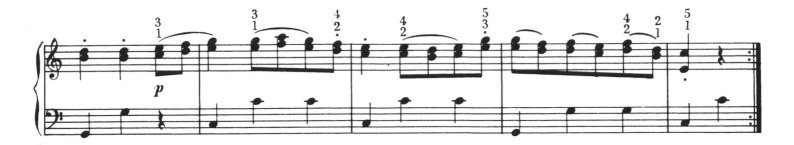

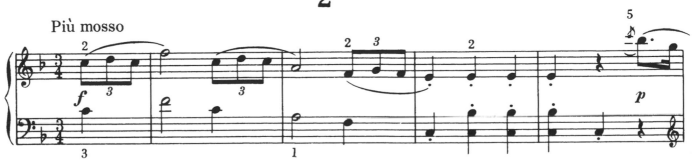

2

Più mosso

Allegro

Wilhelm Friedemann Bach

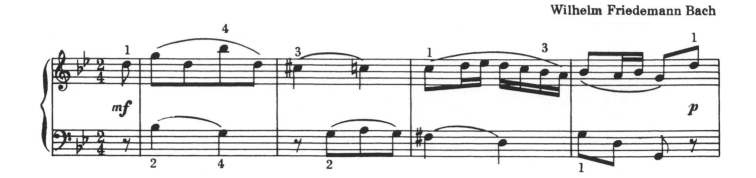

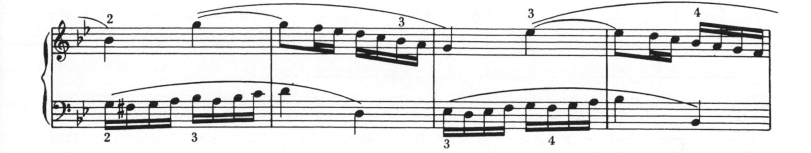

Rondo Espressivo

from a Sonata in B minor

Carl Philipp Emanuel Bach

Andantino cantabile

March

Carl Philipp Emanuel Bach

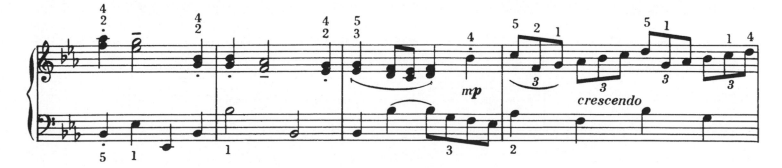

Peasant Dance

Schwaebisch

Johann Christoph Friedrich Bach

Allegretto giocoso

Come, Sweet Death

Johann Sebastian Bach

Arioso

"Largo" from Clavier Concerto in F minor

Johann Sebastian Bach

Andante

*Original key is A♭. In the left hand we incorporated the pizzicato chords of the strings.

© Copyright 1967 Yorktown Music Press, Inc.

Little Prelude

Johann Sebastian Bach

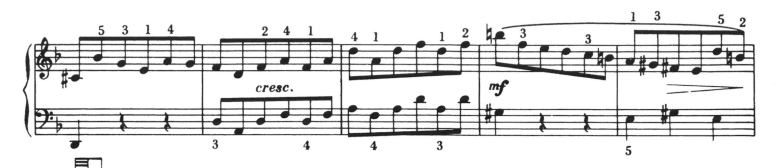

Minuet and Trio

Johann Christoph Friedrich Bach

Allegretto solenne

Trio

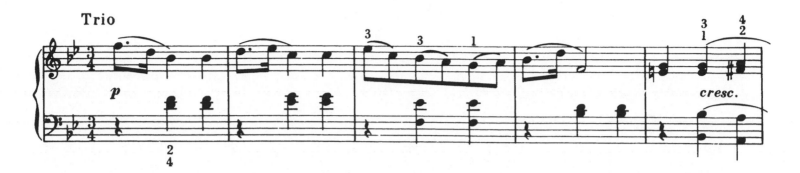

Minuet da Capo

Allemande

Johann Sebastian Bach

Animato

* *Original notation is in sixteenth notes.(From the Notebook for Anna Magdalena Bach)*

Allegretto

from a Fantasia in C

Carl Philipp Emanuel Bach

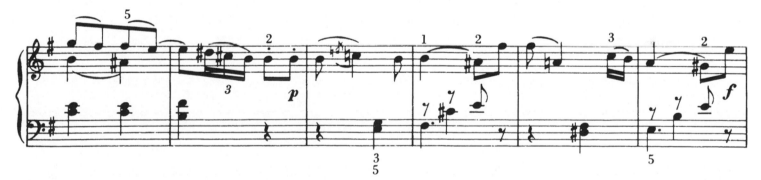

Sarabande

from a Suite in A minor

Johann Sebastian Bach

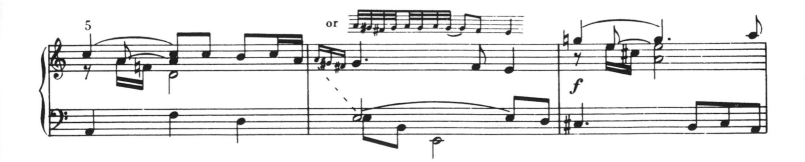

Minuet and Trio

from a Suite in E♭

Johann Sebastian Bach

Con moto

Trio

Andantino

Minuet D.C.

Lamento
from a Sonata in G

Wilhelm Friedemann Bach

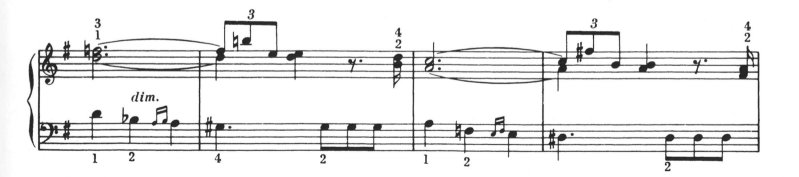

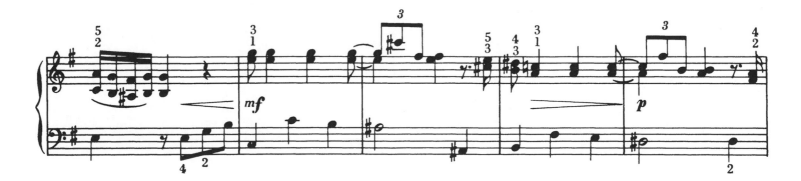

Choral Prelude

"Allein Gott In Der Höh' Sei Ehr"

Johann Christoph Bach
(1642 - 1703)

Moderato

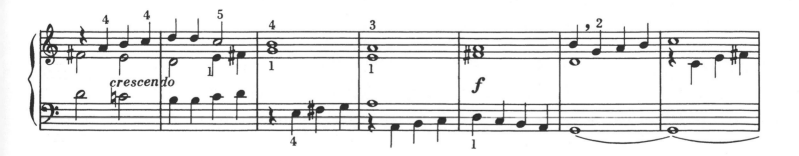

Alla Polacca

Carl Philipp Emanuel Bach

Moderato; ben ritmo

Inventio

Johann Sebastian Bach

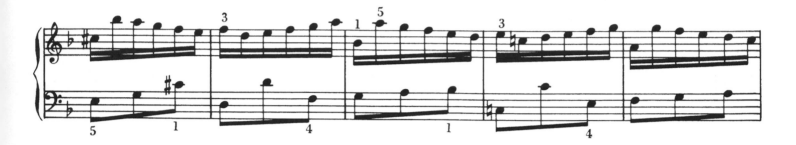

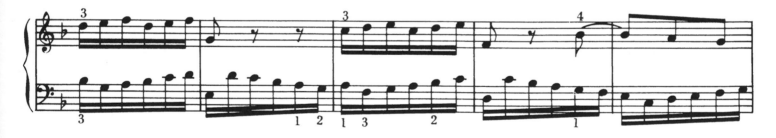

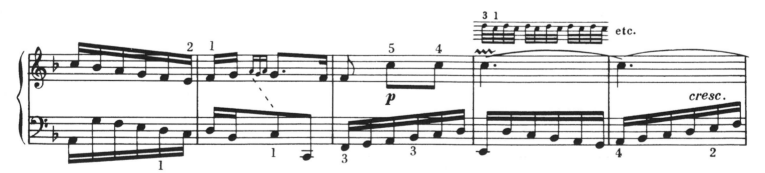

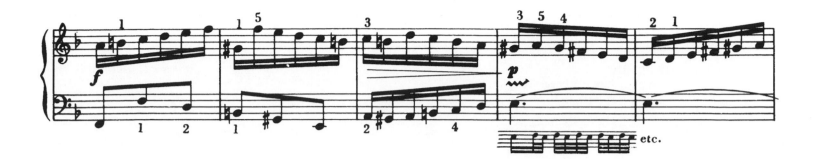

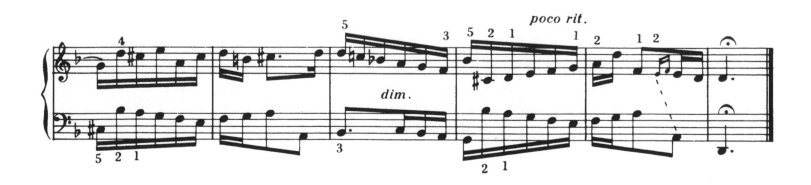

Maggiore e Minore

Minuet and Trio from Sonata op.5 No.2

Moderato

Johann Christian Bach

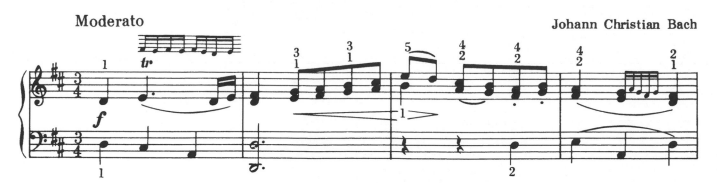

FINE

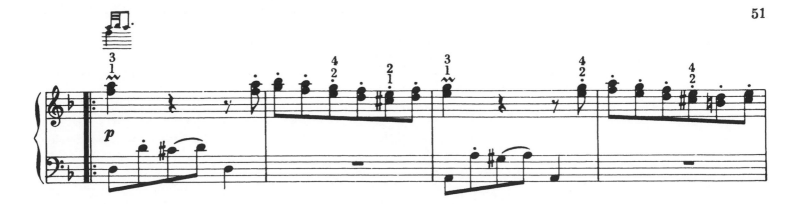

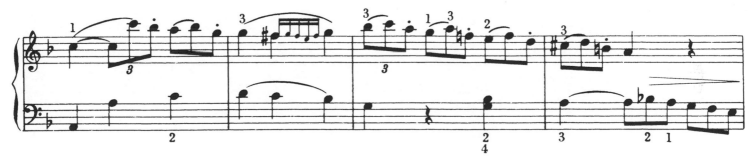

Repeat Magglore
without repetition

Studio

Johann Christoph Friedrich Bach

Bourrée

from a Suite in E♭

Johann Sebastian Bach

Fughetta

Allegretto

Johann Sebastian Bach

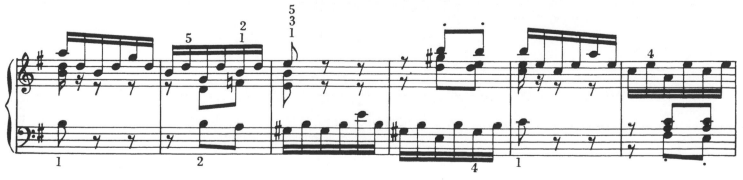

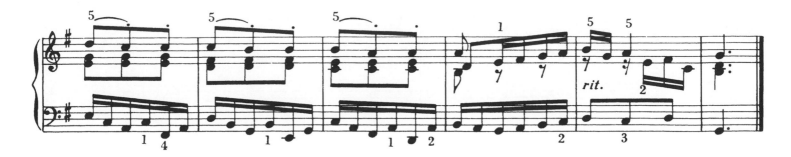

Courante
from French Suite No. 2

Johann Sebastian Bach

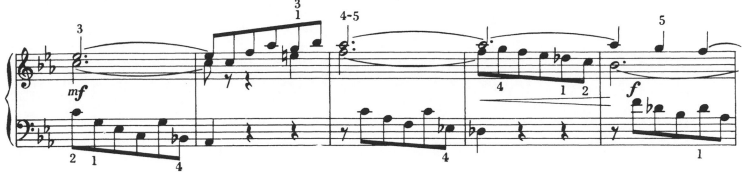

Gavotte and Musette

from English Suite No. 6

Johann Sebastian Bach

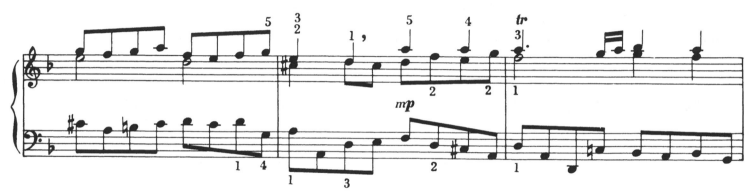

Musette

D.C. Gavotte
without repetitions

Little Prelude

Johann Sebastian Bach

Variations On A French Song

Wilhelm Friedemann Bach

Allegretto

Variation 1

* Dynamic marks in parenthesis refer to repetitions

Variation 2

Variation 3

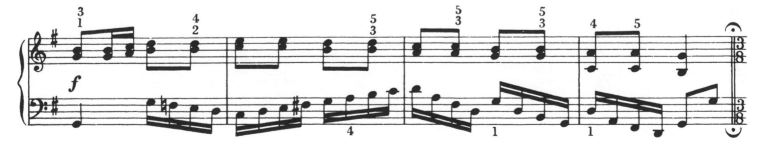

Variation 4 Schwäbisch

Variation 5 alla Siciliana

Variation 6 poco più lento

Variation 7 Allegro

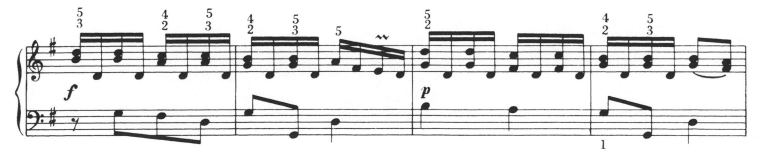

Sinfonia

(Three-voice Invention)

Johann Sebastian Bach

Moderato

p cantabile

Solfeggio

Carl Philipp Emanuel Bach

Canon

from the "Goldberg Variations"

Johann Sebastian Bach

Variations On A Scottish Air,

from Clavier Concerto in B♭ *

Johann Christian Bach

Variation 1

* *Theme and three variations*

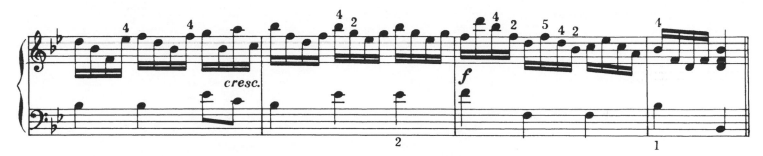

Variation 2

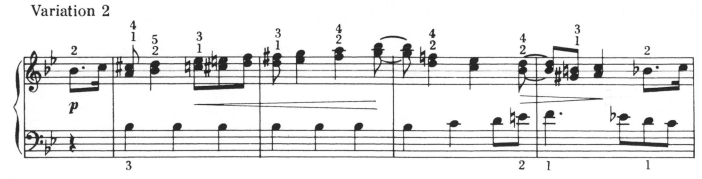

Variation 3

Fughetta

Johann Sebastian Bach

Moderato

Postludium

TRIO from Ouverture in F

Johann Sebastian Bach

Andantino

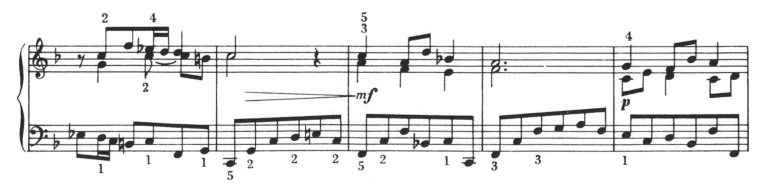